Copyright © 2024 by B. A. Mazur

All rights reserved. No part of this book may be reproduced in any manner whatsoever without written permission except in the case of brief quotations embodied in critical articles and reviews.

"Nine o'Clock, Part II" previously appeared in *Whetstone* of the University of Lethbridge.

First Printing, 2024

Glass Shadows

Glass Shadows

B. A. Mazur

Lily & Sparrow Press

Perhaps in the end
we really were meteors
burning out
somewhere between the stars.

wildflowers

Out of my element here,
Straining my neck to taste familiar sun.
You've brought me to this place to exhibit
your world: rock, lake, sky.
No less beautiful than the land we've come from.
In your kingdom I am a guest,
come to judge mountain views,
test my reflection in eddies of meltwater.
Show me the riches of your palace,
as I test you also.
Wise enough to sit in silence,
mute as we survey the gold.
Such a sun setting so soon.
A stone for a souvenir.
It will last longer than wildflowers
in birth at the edge of the shale.
How long has it been now
since I have been nationalized
into your heartland?

y
o
u
n
g

While we were still young in our marriage,
you took me to the lakes of my fathers—
where I learned to loose my lines in northern waters.
We set sail while the sun and moon traded places,
skipping over darkening waters.
The lake at sundown is a woman in a purple dress,
the moon hanging from her neck.
Lovebird loons cry to stars
while waves make them dance.
You said I carried the lake in my eyes.

c
u
r
v
e

Can I be your daydream for a moment?
The curve at the edge of your mouth.

w
o
n
d
e
r

Call out with wonder,
if that is all you have left.
We are nothing but leaves
dangling between autumn frost
and the hands of the maker.
The colours of the sun alive in our victory:
awake in the face of winter.
This too will come around again.
Exhale like fire,
the space between the stars
hurtling us together again.

c
o
n
c
r
e
t
e

Nine o'clock in the concrete universe.
I am here, alone again.
It is not as unnatural as it seems—
a red heart beating in a gravel cage.
Stagger, come quickly now,
as real as every stubborn gold leaf
on these river guardian trees.
I stumble into you, like the wind
rolling over every contour of these coulee walls.
Tell me if it hurts,
then pray for me—see this the part
of the fairy tale everyone neglects,
the princess and a yellow Indian summer,
irreconciled one to the other.

reprise

Listening to your voice
is to be lulled by the rise and fall of the ocean.
The waves draw me in,
luring me with gentle hums
and promises to share all secrets.
Talk to me in the ways of the moon
playing beneath the water.
A softer consort I should have been.
Bear me out, further from familiar fields,
weaving your reprise with each ripple
around my finger, the midnight halos
that remind us it matters less if I believe you.
All that is cause for joy is the sinking—
deeper and deeper into the gulf you have prepared
for me, creator of all my fancy.
Slip below the depths. Follow if you choose,
our fragility hovering just beneath the surface.

t
h
i
r
s
t

Things I was not ready for:
the waiting.
Not a game, but an ever-present scorching
thirst consuming my whole being.
Lost in the desert.
Three days. Thirty days.
Three hundred days. And death won't come.
Raw. Waiting for a lifetime now,
it seems. I am not the same person
I was when we started out,
confident in our misadventures.
This is a journey, so it must end somewhere,
another coastline where the rocks are not as sharp,
the wind not as hot,
where we come to the end of answered prayers.

e
s
c
a
p
e

No escape for sleeping prey.
Venus arises and we relive the back and forth.
The silent reserve of the final stand.
I hold my breath;
take me for what dreams may come.

afterimage

Life in slow luxury:
come home to wear your shirt,
rest in the indents of your form.
The afterimages that remain
when your key has turned the lock,
footsteps receding down dim hallways
and half-light kisses waiting for brighter days.

a
s
h

Around here we work without shade.
Make our backs one with the sun
carving out dirt while we whittle down the day.
You came in with the crack of a lightning whip.
Smiles like diamonds, kissing dirty hands
that could tell worse stories true.
Never mind if we boast we never heard of you.
Dance me round a little longer, under stars
and under moon. Drink me in a little stronger.
Promise the world, certain to include the ocean.
Hold me by camp light just to sing your devotion.
Watch me fall, deeper still in midnight canyons.
Take the sky when you leave, take your claim.
Fire and water. Ash and rain.
We haven't seen such ghosts since the day you came.

execution

I find I enjoy the idea of you
so much more than the execution.
Isn't that the way of it.
How much more can one person take?

m
a
t
c
h

What I thought was a flame
was just the flicker
of a match burning out.

m
a
r
b
l
e

He could not see
how beautifully fragile she was,
half-formed of marble,
in his dark glasses and white coat.

d
u
s
k

Sometimes you carry the scent of summer.
Your shoulders purple mountains in the dusk.
I'm only left to wonder.

o
s
c
i
l
l
a
t
i
o
n

The first to break the silence
timestamps the date of death.
Is this the aftermath of the divergence?
Caught in perpetual collimation,
from the outside no one would know
what we had forged in transit,
strung from the stars
just to fall asleep.
Is this what you call busy?
The oscillation of descent,
hold onto what you have.
Always running. Always apart.
Always out of reach.
In another hundred thousand years or so
we may reel from the collision.
It would be a lie if I said
I saw this coming.

a
t
t
a
c
k

So discreetly you reached inside
and removed all traces of yourself.
Its not fair to attack when I'm asleep.

q
u
i
e
t

You,
quiet
like clouds
before snow.

distance

If communication is an art form,
we are sketching stick figures.
Long distance postage paid.

sentry

You would forget the moon
if it chose to give up watch.
A lonely sentry
that knows not what my dreams
are made of.

a
f
t
e
r

Catch me lying low in the aftermath,
aftereffect, aftereffect, aftershock,
whatever it was you thought you'd be.
After all, there is nothing more.
I have discharged my duty.
It's the afterimage that stings the most.
Stepping out into the after world of a new day.

f
i
g
h
t

I love you,
even though you are still
a dream, and I am
here fighting
this nightmare.

s
h
a
d
o
w
s

Stranger things, do not even need to tell me.
Lips like chalk, still, it rolls of your tongue.
Words spill and scatter, my lips in a vice.
I did not expect to have to forgive you this early.
The things we put off until we hope it is too late.
You reach out. My body rebels against softer gestures,
drifting out the window, over mulberries into the meadow.
You can't tell shadows the conversations
that should have come easier by now.

mercies

Strange mercies clasped in the cusp of my sternum.
These thoughts catch in my throat.
I must be a cocoon a little longer,
let the light distill further.
Stronger medicine; no cure
for your fingertips brushing back my hair.

c
r
a
d
l
e

Reaching for you
is like holding hands
with the moon,
a dream I cradle
only in my sleep.

surface

When the weight in my chest
becomes so heavy I stay underwater,
quelled by saltwater, you begin
to breath for me. Each exhale
a hand held to the surface.

l
i
g
h
t

In the time of melancholy,
when we slumbered beneath aurora
wondering at our own strange light,
you burst through the replicated pattern
of each day like a gunshot.
Scattered and dazed, I floundered to compile a record
of the sum of all your doings, your belongings.
I was one of them, topping the list with an asterisk.
*Not to be forgotten.

v
a
g
a
b
o
n
d

If home is where the heart is,
then I have no choice
to be anything
but a vagabond.

decipher

I came because I had made a promise.
I had no idea it would be for a funeral,
obvious from almost the first moment.
Alas, it could not be forever.
I had counted you a sister,
standing at the base of the cordillera.
Unable to decipher the language you adopted,
I faded. The consummate professional.
Detached. I suppose somewhere in the subarctic
I'll still answer the phone. And I suppose
you will still be here, or there.
I will come again. Independent.
The other one who never was.
Teen spirit, tires squealing.
Grinding all my gears.

s
u
s
t
a
i
n

I taste the light.
He asks if it sustains me.
I confess I crave
what is lost in shadows.

r
e
m
a
i
n

Sisters of mercy.
The thing I feared the most,
that one day no one could tell
you were ever here,
has come to pass.
I remain, waiting.

h
o
l
l
o
w

Never mine to keep.
Delicate as threads of dandelion seeds
sprinkled in my palm.
Set adrift, the stuff of stars and smoke,
ashes scattered.
Keep your home in the hollow of my chest.
My heart beats for both of us.

enough

Missing you is having a crater for a chest;
even after I stopped believing
my body was not enough to keep you.

s
h
e
l
l

That hollow shell agony
threatens to rip my voice out, again
stabs me in the lungs and heart.
He sits on the edge of the bed,
holding my empty stomach.
Miracles will come.

stories

It is the stories we are not allowed to tell
that are the most important.
The ones that remain tucked in the shadows,
details we whisper only to ourselves,
bring out solitude, turning over in our hands—
precious glassworks in the colour of late evening sun.
Every now and then give a moment's leave to roam
in the blank space between day and night.
Sacred stories preserved for our sanctuary.

soulships

Every once in a while
our soulships pass in the night,
floating on the edge of the moon.
I throw you a line to keep afloat,
but your course never strays.

b
r
e
a
t
h
e

When it is too hard to breathe
you fight my nightmares for me.
That says *I love you* more
than I could whisper.
אהבה

d
r
e
a
m

The rise and fall
of dusk and dawn.
Between such steady respiration
you are still my favourite dream.

h
u
s
h

Peter is asleep in a jail cell and here we are,
all the black and white souls trying to stand up straight.
Slow dancing through shattered glass,
the treason you venerated—
hoped to ignore.
How could I be the one to let you go?
Slipping away in the inferno
a bout of fisticuffs that landed you in the dark.
The stars extinguished by will of force.
Quiet now. Hush with broken arms embrace
daughter-sister kind. The day stills dawns tomorrow.

b
r
e
a
t
h

Sometimes the breath catches in my throat
and I do not know what to make of it.
I wonder if it is all the kisses I had bottled
up for you trying to find their way to Heaven?

h
a
v
e
n

I refuse to go down like this.
Sinking like a dead ship into white coral,
lulled to sleep while sirens whisper narcotic lullabies.
I've carried a pit in my stomach for too long.
Let it tangle me in chains as fine as spiderwebs.
Soft to break until I become the fly.
Meant for greater things, wings less like a moth
and more like an albatross.
Catch currents and set sail over waves wanting to drag me under.
Pray to him to him who walks straight through the churning sea,
calms the roar and quells the hunger in me.
I refuse to go down like this.
A skeleton tucked into someone's closet.
Eyes vacant from the sun,
lungs sucking the life blood from another day,
another revolution, another orbit,
and it all tends to end the same.
Even if now my feet sink
they stepped towards the haven.

e
m
b
e
r
s

Awake to find the sun has bled herself out,
not the only one to stoke fires to keep memories warm.
Lie still, let the last embers soothe
the weight of all the universe in each unsettled joint.
Light comes yellow in the perpetual bliss
of consecutive seconds slipping into each other.
Close your eyes. Perhaps it is not too late.
The grey shadow may rise,
riding on the wind, beckoning you to flee with it.
Take shelter in the basement of unsullied dreams.
The somnambulist carries on a new venture:
perpetual motion, eyes wide open.

d
e
t
r
i
t
u
s

I closed my lips for the full circle of the sun.
Whispered your name to the stars.
Gnawed on the edges of books.
Drank words like poetry
to quench my thirst.
Danced on the edges of clouds.
Laughed at planets spinning out of my grasp.
Slipped, swimming into dreams unrecalled.
Sank, deeper, plummeting into the realm
of sea monsters and siren calls.
Sisters of mercy, waiting in the debris,
hands grasped in prayer. Take me,
drag me out of the detritus
and let what remains emerge.
The monarch from the chrysalis
journey ready.

r
e
v
e
r
i
e

Asleep in the time of war.
And like the sleepwalker, unaware,
unaroused. It should have been a bomb dropping.
An explosion to pry eyes open, watch
the night guard sprawling over concrete.
Scattered somewhere in the secret stories,
fragments of half-forgotten dreams mistook for promises.
She awakens from the reverie with butterfly eyelashes,
slowly, then all at once.

l
i
f
e

Let my life
be your love song
and let hope
carry the rhythm
of each day.

s
a
l
t
w
a
t
e
r

I would send a postcard from my lips to yours,
a greeting from my fingertips long distance postage paid.
It would read: wish you were here,
chasing down Mexican waves, leaving footprints in salt-water froth.
Before the sun slips overboard into the ocean—
my footprints are erased. You are not here to bear witness to this moment.
The only confirmation I was ever really here, fighting the tide:
a colour photograph, a band of white sand and green mountains
outlining bluest water. Blue sky. A great orange orb drowning
in the water, setting me on fire. Your girl suddenly golden
leaving shattered sea shells behind.

y
e
l
l
o
w

In the city, I am alive with anonymity.
She tells me Shabbat shalom
and the blessing is in the rain
carpeting concrete with the first cherry blossoms.
This corner of the park would not be woods enough
for you, even with the cardinal teasing his red belly.
There is room for both of us to fly
in the crowded intimacy of street corners.
Beneath the halo of a yellow umbrella, we are all the wiser.
Home holds my hand, fingers calloused.
Between the sidewalks bloom a daydream for wildflowers.

h
o
m
e

You whisper in the empty spaces
that I am not alone.
It has been so long since I understood
you are my home.

t
o
g
e
t
h
e
r

I wonder if you know how much fire you have put me through.

All the while he whispers, *I love you.*
I will never leave you.
My tears are waves on an ocean we walk together.
You are left behind.

w
a
n
d
e
r

This too is the land of my fathers:
black dirt crowned by boreal woods and a moody sky.
My grandfather would have stories to tell
of this lake and sun, the loons ever moaning a dirge.
They call, and I am awake once more
to the rhythm of each concentric circle testing the waters.
My grandmother is in this country too,
the pixie girl scampering through summer soil,
bare brown toes spinning through the garden.
Her eyes never saw the ocean,
save in the rustle of a barley field.
The rain comes to caress me in my sleep,
whisper this is home and I need not wander.
Even yet, I would trade soft green woods
for a place my mothers' feet never tread.

covenant

I've made a covenant with you,
the map that guides me home.
Some rites of passage come
like the first snowfall.
We who survive the frost are stronger still.

horizon

At the end of day
let me be the horizon
greeting each star
with your praises
on my lips.

s
e
e
d
s

She thinks we rest
somewhere between the stars and the sod,
suspended between sliding second hands
and the descent of the sun.
As she sends dandelion seeds to a mad orbit,
who am I to tell her?

consecrated

Teach me I am consecrated,
that I take up space in your eyes.
Forger of galaxies, my victory
has been established. The fires
I have walked, the coals I have eaten,
have not been a vacant exercise.
Let me not mistake the darkness
for the shadow of your wings.

e
x
h
a
l
e

The rest is now.

Hidden in the secrets that come in the drowsy coolness of staying up too late,

    the pressure against the border of midnight and new days.

You arrive at conclusions like we have been swimming for days,

    treading saltwater in a thousand little anarchies against suspicion.

It comes like the first bit of jagged reef under our feet

and all at once we can exhale.

k
n
o
w
n

I ask God to tell you
I love you.
He says that is all
you have ever known.

For Calvin, and all the dreams we share.

www.ingramcontent.com/pod-product-compliance
Lightning Source LLC
Chambersburg PA
CBHW050225100526
44585CB00017BA/2015